	DATE DUE		

162060

638
HUG
C.1

Hughes, Sarah.

My mom is a
beekeeper

ALICE GUSTAFSON ELEMENTARY LRC

My Family at Work

My Mom Is a Beekeeper

By Sarah Hughes

Children's Press
A Division of Scholastic Inc.
New York / Toronto / London / Auckland / Sydney
Mexico City / New Delhi / Hong Kong
Danbury, Connecticut

Thanks to Vittoria Semproni and Pamlyn and Jake Smith

Photo Credits: Cover and all photos by Maura Boruchow
Contributing Editors: Jeri Cipriano, Jennifer Silate
Book Design: Michael DeLisio

Visit Children's Press on the Internet at:
http://publishing.grolier.com

Library of Congress Cataloging-in-Publication Data

Hughes, Sarah, 1964–
    My Mom is a Beekeeper / by Sarah Hughes.
        p. cm. – (My family at work)
    Includes bibliographical references.
    ISBN 0-516-23181-2 (lib. bdg.) – ISBN 0-516-29577-2 (pbk.)
    1. Bee culture—Juvenile literature. 2. Beekeepers—Juvenile literature. [1. Bee culture.
    2. Beekeepers. 3. Occupations.] I. Title.

SF523.5 .H85 2000
638′.1—dc21

Contents

Hi. I'm Jake.

My mom is a **beekeeper**.

She works with bees.

She wears a **hood** so the bees don't sting her.

Mom keeps her bees in a big box.

The bees live in the box. This is where they make **honey**.

9

Bees make honey from drops of **juice** they get from flowers.

11

We open the big box when it is time to get the honey.

We take a close look.

15

We move the bees.

We get the honey.

I help my mom put the honey in **jars**.

Honey is sweet.

I like honey on bread.

How do you like honey?

21

New Words

beekeeper (**bee**-kee-puhr) a person who takes care
   of bees

honey (**huhn**-ee) the thick sweet liquid made
   by bees

hood (**hood**) a cloth covering for the head and neck

jars (**jarz**) short, wide bottles used to hold things

juice (**joos**) the liquid part of a plant

To Find Out More

Books

Hooray for Beekeeping!
by Bobbie Kalman
Crabtree Publishing

The Life and Times of the Honey Bee
by Charles Micucci
Ticknor & Fields

Web Site

The Honey Expert
http://www.honey.com/kids/
Play games and learn fun facts about honeybees and honey on this
Web site.

Index

About the Author

Sarah Hughes is from New York City and taught school for twelve years. She is now writing and editing children's books. In her free time she enjoys running and riding her bike.

Reading Consultants

Kris Flynn, Coordinator, Small School District Literacy, The San Diego County Office of Education

Shelly Forys, Certified Reading Recovery Specialist, W.J. Zahnow Elementary School, Waterloo, IL

Sue McAdams, Certified Reading Recovery Specialist and Literary Consultant, Dallas, TX